WHEN THE GOING GETS TOUGH

WITH AN INTERACTIVE GUIDE: HELPING CHILDREN FIND THEIR HAPPY

Written By
Dr. Erin Peterson
Illustrated By
Shane Morgan

Printed and bound in the United States of America
First printing • ISBN # 978-1-954463-38-7

WHEN THE GOING GETS TOUGH

WITH AN INTERACTIVE GUIDE: HELPING CHILDREN FIND THEIR HAPPY

Written By
Dr. Erin Peterson
Illustrated By
Shane Morgan

FOR ORDER INFORMATION VISIT

whenthegoinggetstoughguide.com
or
scottpublishingcompany.com

PayPal

MasterCard VISA AMERICAN EXPRESS DISCOVER NETWORK

SCOTT PUBLISHING COMPANY
www.scottpublishingcompany.com
P.O. Box 9707 • Kalispell, MT 59904
Toll Free: 1-800-628-0212
Fax: 1-406-756-0098

DEDICATION

For Everly,

May you always know what a treasure you are! In a world where I'm supposed to be your teacher, it is you who continues to guide and teach me. You have opened my eyes to a larger universe than I knew existed, provided me with deeper perspectives, and motivated me to live my very most favorite life. In spite of your challenges, you choose happiness, which inspires me and this book. Thank you for continuing to share your sweet secrets of life with me. You are a true gift to this world. I am so proud of who you are and love you very much!

Your Biggest Fan,

Mom

WHEN THE GOING GETS TOUGH
WITH AN INTERACTIVE GUIDE:
HELPING CHILDREN FIND THEIR HAPPY
BY DR. ERIN PETERSON

Directions: Scan any QR code below to watch a video where the author discusses the specific benefits of this book for each target audience.

General Public

Families

Educators

Medical Professionals

Mental Health Specialists

I hope you enjoy this book and it becomes a consistent tool for helping the children in your world experience as much happiness in their lifetime as possible! Erin Peterson

A condensed version of this book is also available for purchase:

Both versions can be purchased at whenthegoinggetstoughguide.com

The condensed version includes:

1. **The Story** - This book follows a diverse cast of characters, each sharing their personal strategies for coping with emotions like sadness, stress, anxiety, and frustration.
2. **Discussion Prompts** - These carefully crafted prompts are found throughout the book, at the top of the page. The prompts offer designated moments to pause and engage in meaningful conversations with children about the content you're exploring together.

Note: Pages 1-12 are educational tools provided for the reader, to assist in helping children get the most out of this important topic of emotions (see Table of Contents below for specific educational tools). **To simply read the story, turn to page 13.** **Happy Reading!**

TABLE OF CONTENTS

EDUCATIONAL TOOLS

Background Information

Book Summary: In this book, diverse children express what they have learned to do when feeling emotions such as unhappy, sad, or stressed. Each character reveals a plan of action he or she uses to lift the negative feeling. The characters use the word "reset strategy," leaving the listener with language to use when needing to manage their own feelings.

Purpose: There are two main purposes for this book. First, to provide children with research-based reset strategies and practice in creating their own happiness. That is the goal! Second, to provide adults with the appropriate dialogue to help children process and work through their emotions.

Audience: The intended audience of readers includes, but is not limited to children, educators, pre-service teachers, school staff, therapists, counselors, medical professionals, child-life specialists, daycare providers, social workers, and families. This book is appropriate for any individual wanting to practice reset strategies to manage their emotions, along with adults who would like to do their part as a mental health advocate for children!

Design: The beautiful thing about this book is that it can be adapted to fit the needs of the audience. It can be read to a whole group or one-on-one with a child. It can be read from beginning to end, or in segments so that the focus could simply be practicing one strategy at a time (see Table of Contents for specific strategy page numbers). Once read to children, they can refer back to it with an adult or by themselves whenever necessary. When using the reset strategies, they can be combined and modified to fit the age and interest of the reader. The reset strategies in this book are selected to be practiced when feeling a mix of emotions such as sadness, anxiousness, worry, stress, or anger. Also, there are Reset Strategy Guides (see p. 7-10 and 54-63) included. These guides can be made available to children and referenced as a concrete guide for resetting their emotions before and/or after reading the story.

How to Read this Book with Children: The topic of this book, creating your own happiness, is a lifelong skill and one best learned with adult interaction. I have integrated teaching support throughout this book, removing some of the "guesswork" on how to guide children to step into learning to create their own happiness. The teaching method is called "interactive read aloud" (Barrentine, 1996; Fountas & Pinnell, 2006). Interactive read aloud is when the person reading a book aloud intentionally uses questions and discussion prompts before, during, and after reading. The questions and prompts purposefully guide the children to learn while simultaneously enjoying the story. Throughout the book, I provide ideas for interactions (i.e., questions and prompts) that help the children build an understanding that *even* children, themselves, can learn to manage their emotions. The discussion sets the stage for them to recognize there are plans of action, or reset strategies, they can use to resolve, lift, and move on from feelings of sadness or related emotions.

Need for this Book: According to a recent study conducted by the U.S. Department of Health and Human Services (Lebrun-Harris, Ghandour, Kogan, & Warren, 2022), the number of children (birth to 17 years) diagnosed with mental health conditions has considerably increased in recent years. Specifically, this study found a 27% increase in anxiety and a 24% increase in depression. Children of all ages are faced with many day-to-day challenges in our present world (Deolmi & Pisani, 2020). Studies such as this emphasize the need for more evidence-based resources to assist children in coping with challenges in order to improve their overall health and well-being. This book serves as one of those resources!

Final Thoughts: I believe that, if practiced, these reset strategies will help increase children's feelings of happiness! I do, however, recognize that certain circumstances warrant additional support and expertise. In that case, these strategies can aid in the supplementary work being done elsewhere.

Interactive Read Aloud Description and Prompts

In order to maintain powerful conversations throughout the entire book, you will notice before, during, and after reading discussion prompts (during reading discussion prompts are placed at the top of specific pages throughout the book). These prompts guide you through this book, providing designated places to stop and have important discussions with children about the information you are reading with them. Some prompts are in the form of questions. Other prompts are statements intended to invite children to share their thoughts. You can select the prompts that work for you, add any you feel necessary, and modify to fit the person or group to which you are reading to. Do not feel the need to stop and use every prompt that is provided, as you want to make sure to hold the meaning of the book.

Before Reading Discussion Prompts

1. *Today we are going to read a book about feelings. What are feelings? What are some examples of feelings?*
2. *As human beings, we have all sorts of feelings. Some make us feel good and some make us feel not so good.*
3. *All feelings are important because that means something is going on in our world and in our body.*
4. *This book helps us learn different strategies to try when we are having feelings that may not be so positive, so that we can work to hopefully feel better. That is the goal!*
5. *The book begins with a teacher talking to a group of students. Throughout the book, you will notice that some students will share about reset strategies they like to use to feel better. The book finishes with the teacher talking to the whole group of students again.*
6. *While we read, I encourage you to think about the strategies that you like best and might want to try.*
7. *Optional: A picture walk could take place prior to reading (flipping through the pages without reading to discuss certain things that are taking place in the illustrations).*

Scan QR Code to Download the Interactive Read Aloud Prompts (P. 3-6)

During Reading Discussion Prompts

These prompts are also placed at the top of specific pages throughout the book.

1. *Think in your head or out loud of some things that make you feel happy.* (p.15)
2. *What kinds of things do you feel when you are happy? How do you act when you are happy?* (p.16)
3. *Think in your head or out loud of some things that have made you feel sad.* (p.17)
4. *Has anything in your life made you feel really sad? Would you like to share about it?* (p.18)
5. *What kinds of things do you feel when you are sad? How do you act when you are sad? What are some other types of feelings that make you act this way? Examples include anxious, worried, stressed, and frustrated.* (p.19)
6. *What are some physical clues that someone is feeling sad? Can you always tell on the outside that someone is feeling sad? Explain. What do you think the author means when she says, "Our feelings come and our feelings go"?* (p.20)
7. *Have you ever practiced something really hard and gotten better at it because of that practice? Share about that. That is exactly what you will find with these reset strategies, too. The more you practice them, the better you will become at them.* (p.21)
8. *What does it mean to be mentally strong? Can you think of any examples?* (p.22)
9. *Now we are going to meet children in this story who sometimes feel sad. In the book, they share how they feel and things they try to reset their emotions. Before we do that, let's slow down and talk about what strategies you have used to help you feel better when you are sad. Do you use these strategies for any other types of feelings?* (p.23)
10. *Have you ever tried a breathing technique before? Explain what you did. There are many different types of breathing activities that you could try! It's important to find what works best for you. Let's try this strategy together.* (p.25)
11. *What do you think it means to be present in the moment? What is something you can see, hear, smell, touch, or taste right now?* (p.27)
12. *Why would this strategy make us feel better? What are some things in your life that you are most grateful for?* (p.29)
13. *Why do you think it would be helpful to write or draw about what made you sad?* (p.31)
14. *What do you enjoy doing for exercise? Why are exercise and fresh air so important?* (p.33)
15. *What kind of music do you like? Can you think of an artist or particular song you might*

listen to? Would you prefer to sing and dance or just listen? Have you ever listened really hard to all the words in a song with your eyes closed? It's neat because you get to make your own movie in your mind! (p.35)

16. *Think in your head or out loud of some things you would include in your imaginary world. Who or what would be there and where would you be? Describe it.* (p.37)

17. *Think in your head or out loud of a place you have been that made you really happy. How about a person? A thing? How about a certain time that made you really happy?* (p.39)

18. *Why do you think it is important to choose an adult that you really trust? Think in your head or out loud of an adult who you would feel safe going to when you are feeling sad and want to share about it.* (p.41)

19. *Can anyone think of any other strategies you might want to use when you are wanting to reset your emotions?* (p.42)

20. *Can you think of any other types of feelings you could use these strategies for?* (p.43)

21. *What do you think are some good times throughout the day to check in with yourself?* (p.44)

22. *How do you pay attention to your mood?* (p.45)

23. *What do you think the author means when she says, "It's also important to practice strategies to feel better, so you don't stay there too long"?* (p.46)

24. *Why do you think practicing these strategies is brave?* (p.47)

25. *What do you think it means when the author says, "Resetting your feelings"?* (p.48)

26. *I am so proud of you for all the work you put into reading this book!* (p.49)

After Reading Discussion Prompts

1. *What are some examples of things that could make people around you feel sad? Some of those things may be similar to the reasons you get sad and other times, those things may be different than the reasons you feel sad.*
2. *Which strategy do you think you would be most likely to use when you are feeling sad?*
3. *Which strategy do you think might be the hardest?*
4. *Are there any strategies you could combine and use at the same time?*
5. *You might find that your preference in strategies changes over time, or that you are able to think of ones that are not even in this book.*
6. *The important thing is that you are finding strategies to help you work through your feelings. Because remember, it is okay to feel sad, but you just don't want to stay there too long.*
7. *Some of these strategies can even be practiced without anyone knowing what you are doing. For example, if you are sitting in school and feeling sad, you can take a couple minutes to practice gratitude and think about some things you are most grateful for. No one will even know you are doing it, but hopefully it will help to make you feel better!*
8. *What did you notice about all these characters in the book? What are some things that make them similar? What are some things that make them unique?*
9. *We are all unique in our own ways, but one thing that makes us similar is that we all feel emotions, such as sadness, sometimes. The thing that is making us feel sad may be different, but we all feel it. Reset strategies like the ones in this book can be helpful to anyone no matter where you come from, what you look like, or how old you are.*
10. *Now that we have read this book, I would like you to use it to look back on when you want to practice strategies to feel better. You don't have to read the entire book from front to back each time. You can just flip to whatever strategy you would like to practice and remind yourself about that strategy.*
11. *Finding ways to cope with feelings like sadness is a really important thing to learn and practice. Not everything in life is always going to go like we want it to, but strategies like this can help us get through those times.*
12. *We all want to feel as much happiness as we can in our life. I am proud of you for listening to this book and interacting in order to learn more about feelings and ways to work through your emotions!*

Reset Strategy Description and Guides

The Reset Strategy Guides are tools that can be used before, during, and after reading this book. The purpose of these guides is to assist children in identifying their emotions. In doing so, the guides then help them make a plan to reset an emotion by using one of the strategies introduced in the story. These guides allow the child to better interact with the text and directly apply the important concepts presented in this book. You can select the guides that work best for you and modify them to fit the person or group to whom you are reading to. Each Reset Strategy Guide can be copied off for individual children to complete, projected to an entire group, or used in other ways that work best for a specific environment of readers. The top of each Reset Strategy Guide also includes an explanation that can be used with children, when introducing how to effectively utilize each guide. The end of this book also includes activity guides for children to practice specific reset strategies that are referenced and explained in the story.

Scan QR Code to Download the Reset Strategy Guides (P. 7-10, 54-63)

Before Reading Reset Strategy Guide

Discussion Prompt: *Today we are going to use this guide to help us reflect on how we are feeling. It's important to check in with ourselves by asking, "How am I feeling today?" We will fill in the boxes below by following the arrows on the page. At the end of this guide, we will decide if what we are feeling is something we would like to keep or change. If we decide we would like to try and change what we are feeling, we will make a plan to do that by selecting a Reset Strategy from the story.*

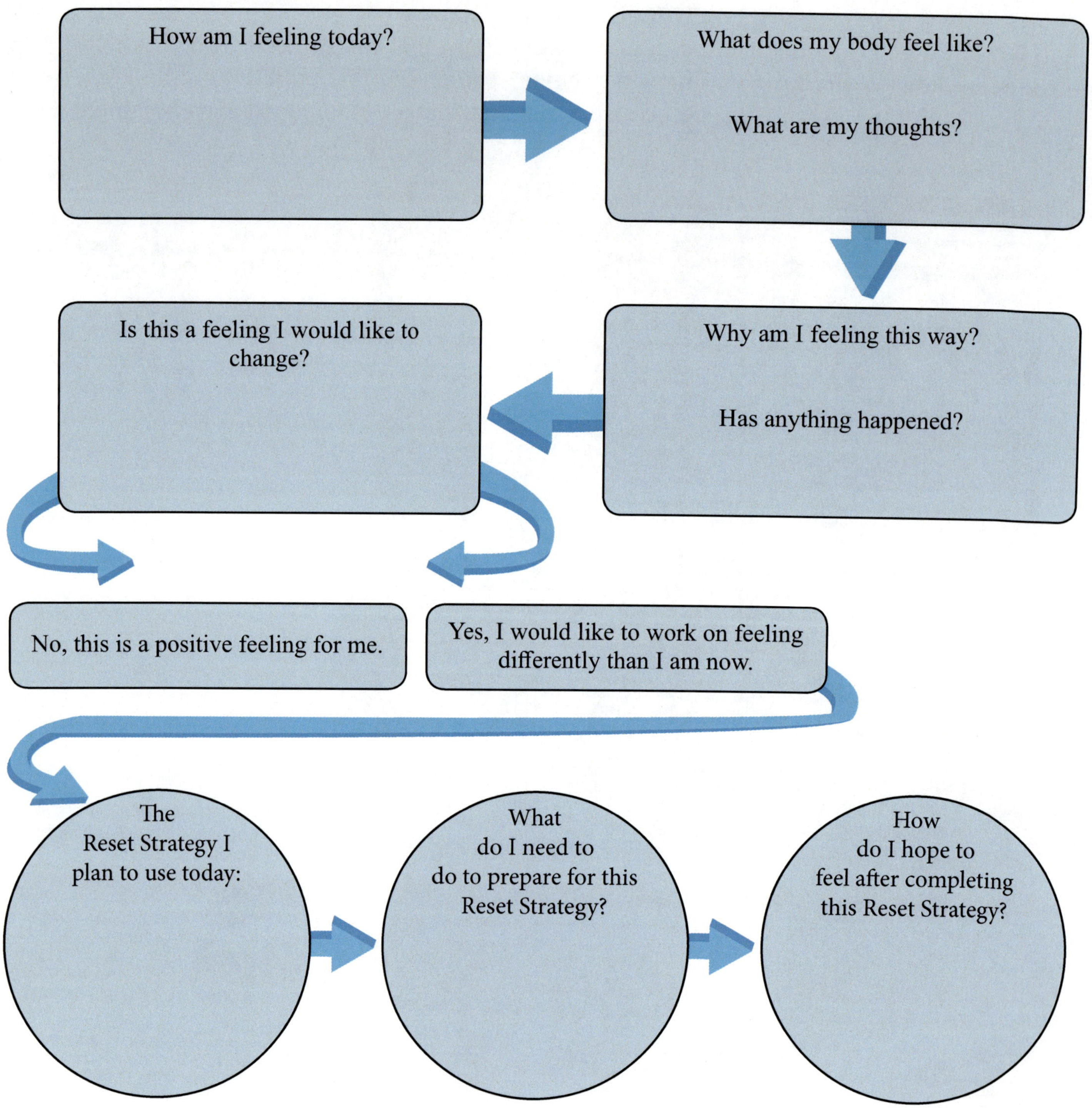

After Reading Reset Strategy Reflection Guide

Discussion Prompt: *Now that we have finished the story and practiced a Reset Strategy, we are going to use this guide to reflect on the strategy. We will start by filling in the first bubble and then follow the arrows to complete the rest.*

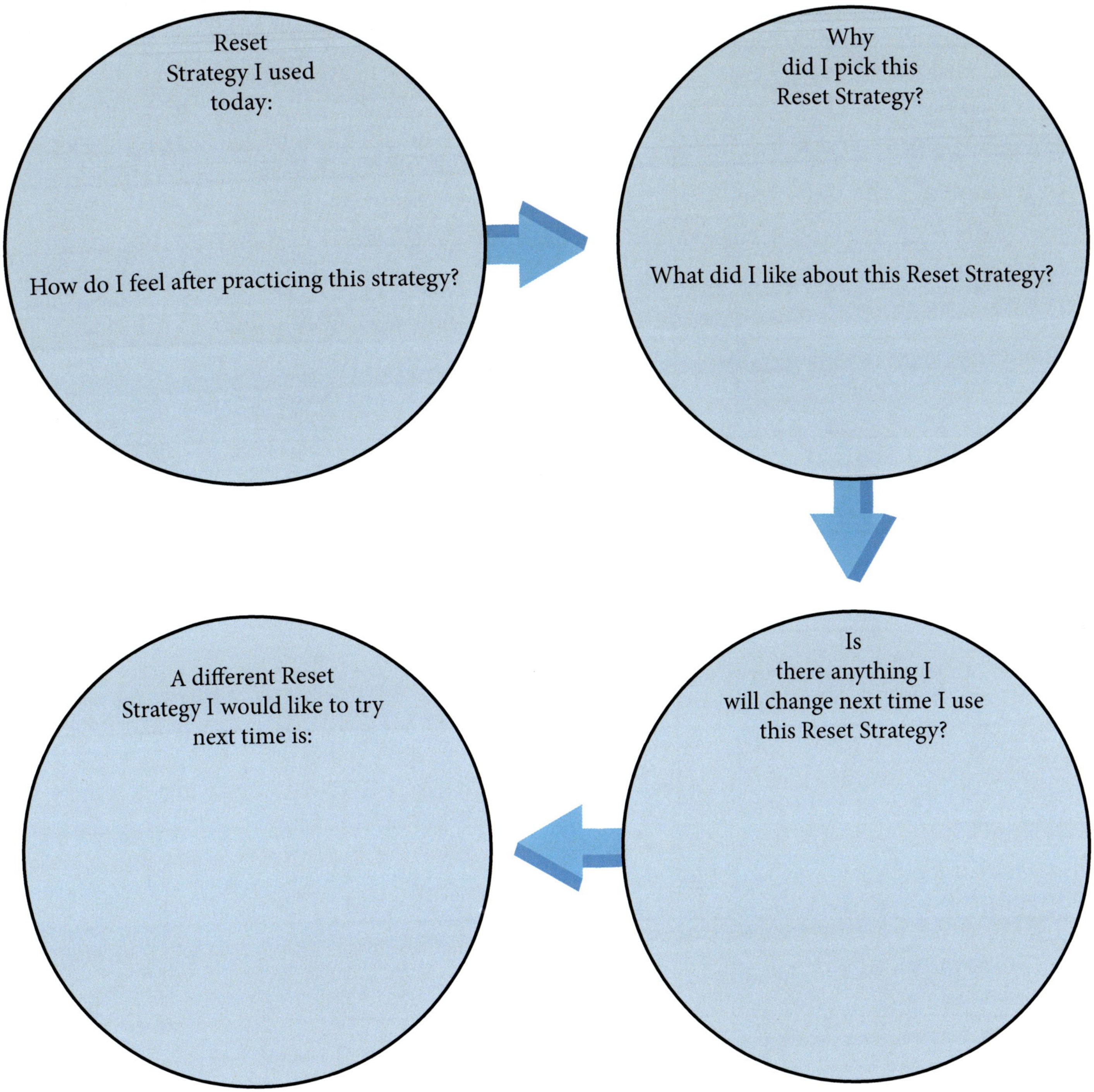

Reset Strategies Choice Guide

Discussion Prompt: *Here is a list of the Reset Strategies that were explained in the book we just read. Whenever you are feeling like you want to reset an emotion you are having, you can look back at this list and remember the strategies we talked about. You can also add any other strategy you have tried to this list, so you don't forget what it is all about. The second column in this guide can be used to mark which strategy you plan to use that day. The third column can be used to record what materials you will need to complete that strategy.*

Reset Strategies	Choice	Materials
1. Breathing Technique		
2. Mindfulness Using Five Senses		
3. Practicing Gratitude		
4. Journaling and Drawing		
5. Exercise and Fresh Air		
6. Music and Movement		
7. Visualization		
8. Guided Imagery		
9. Talking to an Adult		
10. Other:		

Upcoming Companion Curriculum Guide
A Sneak Peek!

As author of the book, *When the Going Gets Tough*, I want to share with you the news that there is a curriculum guide for this book coming soon (2025). I have written the curriculum guide to assist you in helping children recognize and manage their emotions.

The Companion Curriculum Guide consists of a fully developed 15-day unit of study, using *When the Going Gets Tough* as the organizing text for teaching, learning, and emotional growth. Lesson plans for the unit of study incorporate an interactive read aloud, modeling of the emotional reset strategies shared in the storybook, an opportunity for lively practice of the reset strategies, and home-school reflection letters.

More specifically, curriculum components ensure educators are equipped with helpful information to teach about emotional recognition and management with confidence and intentionality. Curricular components include the following:

- **Introductory and Concluding Letters**—Letters written from me to you, the mental health advocate, and to learners and families/caregivers.
- **Introductory and Concluding Surveys**—An optional pre- and post-survey set up to assess children's progress and gather individual and group assessment information.
- **Curriculum Calendar**—A guide to help plan the unit. Sessions can be taught in a 15-day block or spread out over time. Lesson sequence is somewhat flexible. For these reasons, a planning calendar is a practical curriculum tool.
- **Lesson Plans**—Fifteen individual lesson plans are described in detail. They use the reliable workshop approach: mini-lesson, activity time, and share time. Lesson extensions support planning and teaching as well.
- **Morning Meeting Plans**—Fifteen individual morning meeting plans are described in detail. Each morning meeting session, coincides with the lesson plan topic for that day. Morning meeting plans include a student message, greeting, activity, and share opportunity.
- **Coloring Book**—The nine characters children meet in the book, *When the Going Gets Tough*, are revisited in the form of a coloring book.
- **Home Link**—To bridge school and home, Home Link letters are provided to copy and send home with the completion of each lesson. The letters encourage families/caregivers to discuss emotional awareness and management, using language and information offered in the curriculum.

To find out when and where this Companion Curriculum Guide is available, please visit my website at whenthegoinggetstoughguide.com

Resources

Barrentine, S.J. (1996). Engaging with reading through interactive read-alouds. *The Reading Teacher, 50*(1), p. 36-43.

Children's Healthcare of Atlanta. Healthy coping strategies for kids. *Strong4Life*. Retrieved June 24, 2024, from https://www.strong4life.com/en/emotional wellness/coping/healthy-coping-strategies-for-kids

Children's Hospital, Colorado. Pediatric coping skills. *The Pediatric Mental Health Institute*. Retrieved June 24, 2024, from https://www.childrenscolorado.org doctors-and-departments/departments/psych/mental-health-professional-resources primary-care-articles/pediatric-coping-skills/

Deolmi M. & Pisani F. Psychological and psychiatric impact of COVID-19 pandemic among children and adolescents. *Acta Biomed*, Retrieved June 24, 2024, from https://www.ncbi.nlm.nih.gov/pmc/articles/PMC7927507/

Fountas, I.C., & Pinnell, G. (2006). *Teaching for comprehending and fluency: Thinking, talking, and writing about reading, K–8.* Portsmouth, NH: Heinemann.

Lebrun-Harris, L.A., Ghandour, R.M., Kogan, M.D., Warren, M.D. Five year trends in US children's health and well-being, 2016-2020. *JAMA Pediatrics*, Retrieved June 24, 2024, from https://jamanetwork.com/journals/jamapediatricsfullarticle/2789946

Morin, A. (2020). 15 Coping strategies for kids. *Very Well Family*. Retrieved June 24, 2024, from https://www.verywellfamily.com/coping-skills-for-kids-4586871

WHEN THE GOING GETS TOUGH

WITH AN INTERACTIVE GUIDE: HELPING CHILDREN FIND THEIR HAPPY

Written By
Dr. Erin Peterson
Illustrated By
Shane Morgan

Before Reading Discussion Prompts

1. *Today we are going to read a book about feelings. What are feelings? What are some examples of feelings?*
2. *As human beings, we have all sorts of feelings. Some make us feel good and some make us feel not so good.*
3. *All feelings are important because that means something is going on in our world and in our body.*
4. *This book helps us learn different strategies to try when we are having feelings that may not be so positive, so that we can work to hopefully feel better. That is the goal!*
5. *The book begins with a teacher talking to a group of students. Throughout the book, you will notice that some students will share about reset strategies they like to use to feel better. The book finishes with the teacher talking to the whole group of students again.*
6. *While we read, I encourage you to think about the strategies that you like best and might want to try.*
7. *Optional: A picture walk could take place prior to reading (flipping through the pages without reading to discuss certain things that are taking place in the illustrations).*

Discussion Prompt: *Think in your head or out loud of some things that make you feel happy.*

There are many things in life that can make us feel happy, like jumping in puddles or spending time with someone we love.

Discussion Prompts: *What kinds of things do you feel when you are happy? How do you act when you are happy?*

Feeling happy can make us smile and feel all warm and fuzzy inside.

Discussion Prompt: *Think in your head or out loud of some things that have made you feel sad.*

Yet, just like things that can make us feel happy, there are things that can make us feel sad, too. Losing a game, missing someone, or feeling left out, may bring sadness.

Discussion Prompts: *Has anything in your life made you feel really sad? Would you like to share about it?*

Sometimes we can even feel super sad, like if we move to a new place, when someone we love is in the hospital, or if we lose a pet.

Discussion Prompts: *What kinds of things do you feel when you are sad? How do you act when you are sad? What are some other types of feelings that make you act this way? Examples include anxious, worried, stressed, and frustrated.*

**When we are sad, we might feel quiet and want to be alone.
We might even feel like crying.**

Discussion Prompts: *What are some physical clues that someone is feeling sad? Can you always tell on the outside that someone is feeling sad? Explain. What do you think the author means when she says, "Our feelings come and our feelings go"?*

It is okay to feel sad sometimes. It's part of life. But like the clouds in the sky or the waves in the ocean, our feelings come and our feelings go.

Discussion Prompts: *Have you ever practiced something really hard and gotten better at it because of that practice? Share about that. That is exactly what you will find with these reset strategies, too. The more you practice them, the better you will become at them.*

When the going gets tough, and we are feeling sad, there are strategies we can practice in order to work through our feelings. Strategies are like a "game plan" or "action plan" we can learn and then use to help us change what's happening in our head and with our mood. We call these reset strategies because they help us reset our feelings.

Discussion Prompts: *What does it mean to be mentally strong?*
Can you think of any examples?

To stay healthy, our bodies need exercise, and so does our brain. Learning and practicing these reset strategies can help us to feel mentally strong.

Discussion Prompts: *Now we are going to meet children in this story who sometimes feel sad. In the book, they share how they feel and things they try to reset their emotions. Before we do that, let's slow down and talk about what strategies you have used to help you feel better when you are sad. Do you use these strategies for any other types of feelings?*

What are some strategies you use when the going gets tough and you feel sad?

Reset Strategy 1: Breathing Technique

Fun Facts about Emily:

- Loves acting and painting
- Is an only child
- Enjoys baking cookies
- Favorite food is spaghetti
- Wants to be a veterinarian

Hi! I'm Emily. When I'm feeling sad, I practice my breathing.

Discussion Prompts: *Have you ever tried a breathing technique before? Explain what you did. There are many different types of breathing activities that you could try! It's important to find what works best for you. Let's try this strategy together.*

I close my eyes and relax my body and my brain. I take a deep breath through my nose and feel the air fill up my belly. Then, I slowly blow all the air out through my mouth. I do this a couple times in a row until I start to feel better.

Reset Strategy 2: Mindfulness Using Five Senses

Fun Facts about Antonne:
- Likes to read
- Won a Spelling Bee in school
- Favorite food is pizza
- Volunteers at the Humane Society
- Has five siblings

Hey there, my name is Antonne. Sometimes I feel sad. When I do, I use my five senses so I can be present in the moment.

Discussion Prompts: *What do you think it means to be present in the moment? What is something you can see, hear, smell, touch, or taste right now?*

I use my eyes to notice the interesting things around me, my ears to hear any unique sounds, my nose to notice smells that I enjoy, and my hands to feel the different textures of things around me. Sometimes, I even take a bite or drink of something so I can think about what I am tasting!

Reset Strategy 3: Practicing Gratitude

Fun Facts about Jacob:
- Plays guitar
- Lives with his grandparents
- Loves winter
- Favorite color is green
- Won a medal for bowling in the Special Olympics

My name is Jacob. Do you know that when I am feeling unhappy, it helps to think about the things I am grateful for?

Discussion Prompts: *Why would this strategy make us feel better? What are some things in your life that you are most grateful for?*

I am grateful for my family, my friends, my school, and my home. I think about all the reasons I am grateful for these things and when I do, I start to feel better!

Reset Strategy 4: Journaling and Drawing

Fun Facts about Mika:
- Has two sisters
- Loves to play soccer
- Favorite treat is ice cream
- Is homeschooled
- Helps at his parents' bakery

Hello, I'm Mika. Journaling is one thing that helps when my body is feeling sad.

Discussion Prompt: *Why do you think it would be helpful to write or draw about what made you sad?*

Sometimes I write about what is making me sad, and other times I write about something completely different. I also like to draw pictures to go along with my writing.

Reset Strategy 5: Exercise and Fresh Air

Fun Facts about Miya:
- Plays softball
- Likes to travel
- Has a pet bunny
- Teaches sign language to others
- Writes books

Hey, I'm Miya. Yesterday when I was feeling sad, I decided to get some exercise and fresh air.

Discussion Prompts: *What do you enjoy doing for exercise?*
Why are exercise and fresh air so important?

I walked around my neighborhood two times. While I was walking, I looked at everything around me, like the trees, the houses, and the birds. The sun felt really nice shining down on my face. It warmed up my whole body!

Reset Strategy 6: Music and Movement

Fun Facts about Aleena:
- Moved to a new town in 1st grade
- Spends a lot of time in nature
- Enjoys cooking
- Likes to camp in the summertime
- Just learned to ride a bike

When things in my life feel hard, I use music to make me feel better.
I'm Aleena, by the way!

Discussion Prompts: *What kind of music do you like? Can you think of an artist or particular song you might listen to? Would you prefer to sing and dance or just listen? Have you ever listened really hard to all the words in a song with your eyes closed? It's neat because you get to make your own movie in your mind!*

I put my headphones on and play my very favorite songs. Sometimes the songs are fast and sometimes they are slow. Sometimes I dance and sometimes I sing. I also like to close my eyes and think about the words that are playing. If I concentrate really hard, I can see the song playing out like a movie!

Reset Strategy 7: Visualization

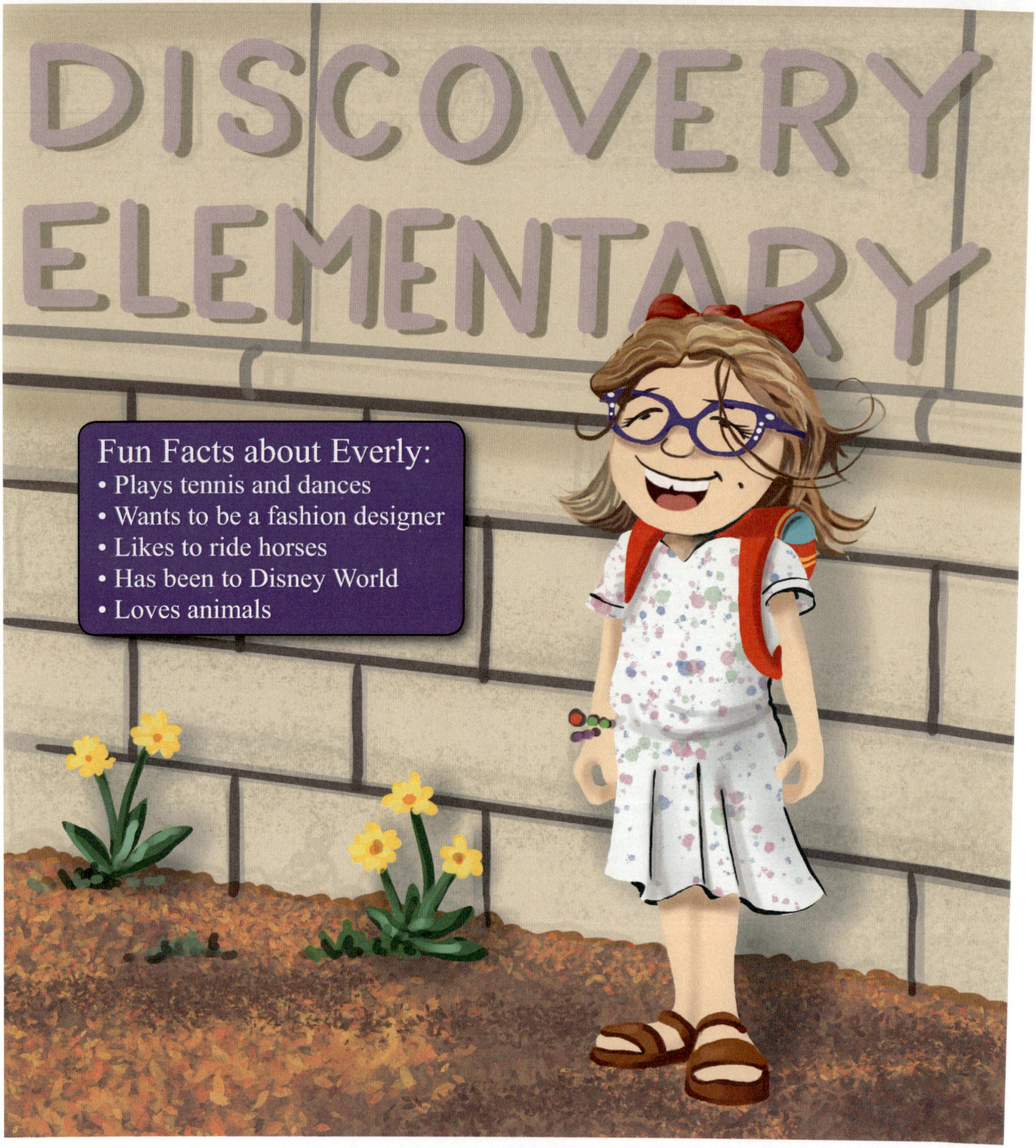

My name is Everly and I like to visualize, or picture, my own world in my head when I want to feel happier. Sometimes I even like to draw what that world looks like!

Discussion Prompts: *Think in your head or out loud of some things you would include in your imaginary world. Who or what would be there and where would you be? Describe it.*

My imaginary world has flying unicorns and pink and purple zebras that talk. Everything in this world is colorful and exciting. It's all really magical!

Reset Strategy 8: Guided Imagery

Fun Facts about Mateo:
- Has a dog named Leo
- Loves the lake
- Collects rocks
- Enjoys playing card games
- Does magic tricks

Hi, nice to meet you! I'm Mateo. When I am feeling down, I like to reflect on something that makes me really happy.

Discussion Prompts: *Think in your head or out loud of a place you have been that made you really happy. How about a person? A thing? How about a certain time that made you really happy?*

It may be a place I have been, a person or thing in my life, or a certain time that made me feel really great. I close my eyes and think about as many details as I can. The other day I thought about the trip my family took to the lake. I used my mind's eye to remember the campfires we had, the games we played, and the boat rides we took. We laughed a lot on that trip!

Reset Strategy 9: Talking to an Adult

Howdy! My name is Jordan. I like to talk with an adult I trust when I want to feel better about something.

Discussion Prompts: *Why do you think it is important to choose an adult that you really trust? Think in your head or out loud of an adult who you would feel safe going to when you are feeling sad and want to share about it.*

Yesterday, I talked to my mom and she helped me figure out my feelings. I also like to talk with my teacher at school and my grandparents on the phone. They all listen to what I have to say and find ways to make me feel better.

Discussion Prompt: *Can anyone think of any other strategies you might want to use when you are wanting to reset your emotions?*

Thank you all for sharing! Those are wonderful reset strategies to use when you are feeling sad.

Discussion Prompt: *Can you think of any other types of feelings you could use these strategies for?*

Did you know that you can use these strategies not only when you are feeling sad, but when you are feeling other emotions like anxious, worried, stressed, or frustrated?

Discussion Prompt: *What do you think are some good times throughout the day to check in with yourself?*

All of these emotions can feel very overwhelming. It's important to check in with yourself by asking, "How am I feeling today?"

Discussion Prompt: *How do you pay attention to your mood?*

Pay attention to your mood. When you aren't feeling right, figure out what you need to feel better.

Discussion Prompt: *What do you think the author means when she says, "It's also important to practice strategies to feel better, so you don't stay there too long"?*

Remember, it's okay to feel sad sometimes. It's also important to practice strategies to feel better, so you don't stay there too long. The more you practice reset strategies like these, the better you will become at them.

Discussion Prompt: *Why do you think practicing these strategies is brave?*

Make sure to celebrate yourself afterwards, because you just did a really brave and important thing! You made yourself feel better.

Discussion Prompt: *What do you think it means when the author says, "Resetting your feelings"?*

Resetting your feelings is not always going to be easy, but you are powerful and strong! You can do hard things.

Discussion Prompt: *I am so proud of you for all the work you put into reading this book!*

When the going gets tough, you have the reset strategies to keep going!

After Reading Discussion Prompts

1. *What are some examples of things that could make people around you feel sad? Some of those things may be similar to the reasons you get sad and other times, those things may be different than the reasons you feel sad.*

2. *Which strategy do you think you would be most likely to use when you are feeling sad?*

3. *Which strategy do you think might be the hardest?*

4. *Are there any strategies you could combine and use at the same time?*

5. *You might find that your preference in strategies changes over time, or that you are able to think of ones that are not even in this book.*

6. *The important thing is that you are finding strategies to help you work through your feelings. Because remember, it is okay to feel sad, but you just don't want to stay there too long.*

7. *Some of these strategies can even be practiced without anyone knowing what you are doing. For example, if you are sitting in school and feeling sad, you can take a couple minutes to practice gratitude and think about some things you are most grateful for. No one will even know you are doing it, but hopefully it will help to make you feel better!*

8. *What did you notice about all these characters in the book? What are some things that make them similar? What are some things that make them unique?*

9. *We are all unique in our own ways, but one thing that makes us similar is that we all feel emotions, such as sadness, sometimes. The thing that is making us feel sad may be different, but we all feel it. Reset strategies like the ones in this book can be helpful to anyone no matter where you come from, what you look like, or how old you are.*

10. *Now that we have read this book, I would like you to use it to look back on when you want to practice strategies to feel better. You don't have to read the entire book from front to back each time. You can just flip to whatever strategy you would like to practice and remind yourself about that strategy.*

11. *Finding ways to cope with feelings like sadness is a really important thing to learn and practice. Not everything in life is always going to go like we want it to, but strategies like this can help us get through those times.*

12. *We all want to feel as much happiness as we can in our life. I am proud of you for listening to this book and interacting in order to learn more about feelings and ways to work through your emotions!*

Reader Testimonials

As an elementary principal, I am proud to recommend this book as a valued addition to every school classroom and library. This beautifully crafted children's book is a powerful tool for helping young readers to recognize and understand their emotions. Through its relatable characters and engaging examples, children can see themselves on every page. Each character offers practical reset strategies, providing children with positive examples of how to navigate their feelings. The kid-friendly examples and relatable storytelling make complex emotions accessible and understandable for young learners. The prompts on each page make each page interactive, sparking meaningful discussions and encouraging deeper reflection. This book doesn't just teach; it fosters an environment where kids can openly talk about their emotions and learn from them.

This book is an inspiring reminder that even when the going gets tough, choosing happiness is always an option. It's a must-have resource for any parent, educator, medical provider or therapist who is dedicated to nurturing emotionally intelligent and resilient children.

Ali Parkinson
Elementary Principal

In a world where our future teachers need to be prepared for much more than teaching content to their students, this book provides the necessary tools, strategies, and conversation starters to support students from all backgrounds. Everything from relatable characters to real-life scenarios to questions that will get students thinking and talking makes this book a "must read" for students and teachers in today's classrooms.

Dr. Sonja Brandt
Professor of Higher Education (Teaching and Learning)

As both a parent and an educator, fostering emotional intelligence in children and teachers is critical. 'When the Going Gets Tough' is a true gem—it equips children (and their teachers) with practical strategies to navigate complex emotions and find their happiness. This beautifully written and illustrated book not only captured my children's imaginations, but also sparked meaningful conversations about handling difficult emotions. A must-have for every home and classroom library!

Dr. Brittany Hagen
Parent
Professor of Higher Education (Teacher Education)

How do we as adults support children as they face new emotional experiences every day? In this engaging and inspiring book, Dr. Peterson paves the way for us to teach children about their emotional lives. She artfully uses the interactive read aloud method to support adults as they read the book with children. Throughout the book she integrates meaningful interaction prompts to invite before, during and after reading discussion. Children get to engage with characters in the book by naming, validating and resetting negative emotions. Because children can see themselves in Dr. Peterson's resilient characters, they make personal connections to them. This supports them as they "try out" resetting their own emotions as they encounter new experiences daily. The joyful characters set the tone for turning frowns into smiles but not by "stuffing" emotions. Rather, children learn to intentionally select strategies from a toolbox and to take charge of their emotional lives in developmentally appropriate ways.

Dr. Shelby Barrentine
Professor Emerita
Interactive Read Aloud Specialist

A book like "When the Going Gets Tough" is exactly what our children need, offering them tools to find their joy amidst life's challenges. This interactive read-aloud, complete with guiding questions for the teacher or parent, provides simple effective strategies that empower young readers to regulate their emotions and find their happy. It's an invaluable resource that every educator and parent should have in their toolkit.

Jana Makovsky
Elementary Education Teacher and Instructional Coach

As an elementary school teacher, I believe this book is a game-changer for educators and children alike. It equips adults with tools to help kids handle tough moments and embrace their emotions. By teaching kids it's okay to feel deeply and offering practical "reset strategies," it provides both teachers and students with the skills to navigate big emotions. The diverse characters allow kids to feel represented, and its colorful, engaging illustrations will draw readers of all ages in! Teaching children to navigate difficulties with confidence ensures they grow into resilient and emotionally healthy humans. This book is a must-have for every classroom and anyone working with children.

Kathleen Pedersen
Elementary Education Teacher and Reading Specialist

This book needs to be in every home that has a child, all schools, and all libraries! What an excellent resource for all children, and their families, to help them navigate through life's mental and physical challenges!

Dr. Eric Lunn
Pediatrician
Former Hospital President
School Board Member
School of Medicine & Health Sciences Faculty Member

Dr. Erin Peterson beautifully addresses the complexity of self-regulation of emotions. The strategies are presented in an imaginative and effortless manner. "When The Going Gets Tough" undoubtedly guides adults and children in communicating about feelings effectively. The Interactive Guide will positively impact the mental health of children and assist adults in navigating communication to help the child find their happy.

Julie Riddle LICSW, LCSW, MSW
Owner & Clinician
Adjunct Professor

About the Author

Erin, along with her two younger siblings, was born and raised in beautiful Bemidji, Minnesota. Growing up in a family of educators, she recognized the value of a quality education and chose to pursue teaching as well. Erin graduated from the University of North Dakota (UND) with a Bachelor's degree in Elementary Education and a minor in mathematics. During this time, she was also part of the UND women's tennis team. Upon graduation, she taught fourth grade, while also completing her Master's degree through a first year teacher/mentoring program. Erin then taught eight years in fifth grade before receiving her PhD in Education, with an emphasis in literacy. Erin has a true passion for education and has loved every role she has played in the past 17 years, including student teacher, substitute teacher, elementary teacher, cooperating teacher, paraprofessional, tennis coach, standardized physical exam teaching associate, and adjunct faculty member. She has fourteen years experience teaching various literacy courses in the Education Department at the University of North Dakota as an adjunct faculty member.

Erin welcomed the birth of her amazing daughter, Everly, in 2015. Shortly after birth, Everly was diagnosed with an extremely rare syndrome called Megacystis Microcolon Intestinal Hypoperistalsis Syndrome (MMIHS). For more information on this syndrome, please visit mmihs.org. MMIHS affects the motility of the bladder and gastrointestinal system and is tremendously complex. Erin's daily roles with Everly, beyond mom, have included primary medical caretaker, advocate, teacher, and one-on-one paraprofessional, to name a few. She has spent time in the U.S. Capitol and at other various large-scale medical conferences advocating for rare diseases such as MMIHS. She is also the vice president of the MMIHS non-profit organization, founded in 2017 by Everly's Aunt, Mollie Caspers. Erin's experience with Everly has opened a whole new world of education, allowing her to think beyond the walls of a classroom. This children's book is one example of that!

A Note from the Author: *My inspiration for this book is a combination of all that my daughter and these other educational experiences have taught me. I am thrilled to share it with the world and believe it will have a positive impact on the mental well-being of children everywhere!*

For more information on Erin and related topics, please visit her accounts:

Email: embracedbyerin@gmail.com
Web: whenthegoinggetstoughguide.com
Blog: embracedbyerin.com
Pinterest: embracedbyerin
Facebook: embracedbyerin
Instagram: embracedbyerin
YouTube: embracedbyerin
TikTok: embracedbyerin

Reset Strategy
Activity Guides

Scan QR Code to Download the Reset Strategy Guides (P. 7-10, 54-63)

Directions: Use the following activity guides to practice specific reset strategies that are referenced and explained in the story, *When the Going Gets Tough* by Dr. Erin Peterson.

Reset Strategy 1: Breathing Technique (Emily, p. 24-25)

I Can Statement: *Like Emily, I can practice my* <u>*breathing technique*</u> *as a reset strategy to help manage my emotions!*

Directions: Use the picture below to practice taking deep breaths in and deep breaths out. Follow one rainbow ring at a time. Repeat as many times as you would like.

Breathing Technique

Rainbow Breathing

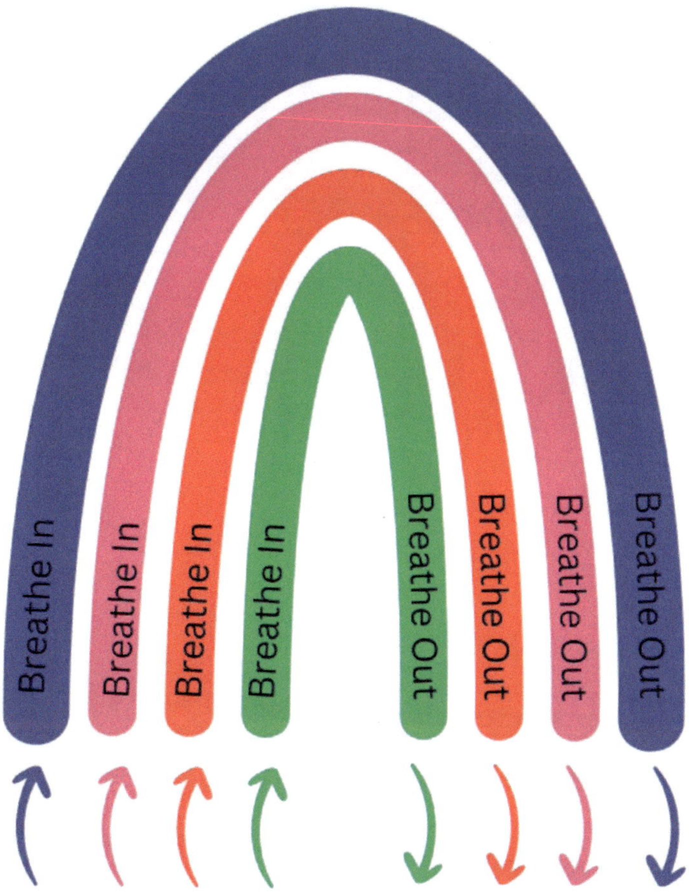

Reset Strategy 2: Mindfulness Using Five Senses (Antonne, p. 26-27)

I Can Statement: *Like Antonne, I can practice* <u>*mindfulness using my five senses*</u> *as a reset strategy to help manage my emotions!*

Directions: Use the guide below to practice using your five senses as a mindfulness technique to help you stay in the moment and notice everything around you.

Mindfulness Using Five Senses

5 - 4 - 3 - 2 - 1

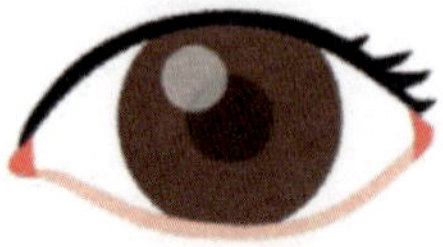

5 THINGS I CAN SEE

4 THINGS I CAN FEEL

3 THINGS I CAN HEAR

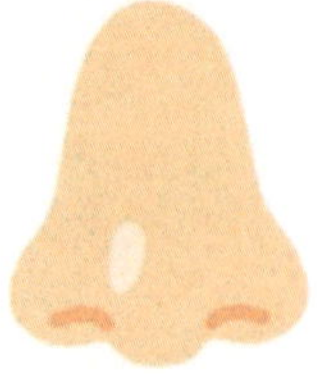

2 THINGS I CAN SMELL

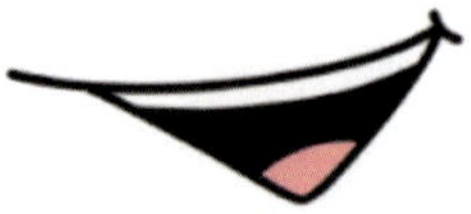

1 THING I CAN TASTE

Reset Strategy 3: Practicing Gratitude (Jacob, p. 28-29)

I Can Statement: *Like Jacob, I can practice gratitude as a reset strategy to help manage my emotions!*

Directions: Write the things you are grateful for in and around the gratitude jar below. See how full you can make it.

Practicing Gratitude

Gratitude Jar

Reset Strategy 4: Journaling and Drawing (Mika, p. 30-31)

I Can Statement: *Like Mika, I can practice* *journaling and drawing* *as a reset strategy to help manage my emotions!*

Directions: Using your own paper and writing utensils, choose a prompt below to journal and draw about. Use as many prompts as you would like, or make up your own.

Journaling and Drawing

Writing Prompts

What makes you really happy?	How can you spread kindness?	What are your favorite things to do?
What do you do when you are feeling sad?	When was a time you felt hurt? What happened?	What is one thing you would like to write about?
What is one of your favorite memories?	When was a time you felt really angry?	What is on your mind right now?

Reset Strategy 5: Exercise and Fresh Air (Miya, p. 32-33)

I Can Statement: *Like Miya, I can get <u>exercise and fresh air</u> as a reset strategy to help manage my emotions!*

Directions: Roll a dice and complete the exercise that is next to the number you rolled. Repeat as many times as you would like. In order to get fresh air at the same time, these exercises can be practiced outside (if possible).

<u>Exercise and Fresh Air</u>

<u>Exercise Dice</u>

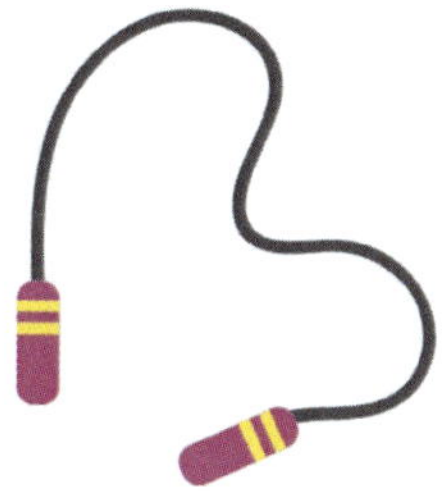

 DO 10 SQUATS

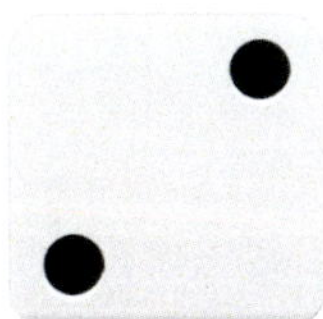 RUN IN PLACE FOR 1 MINUTE

 JUMP UP AND DOWN 10 TIMES

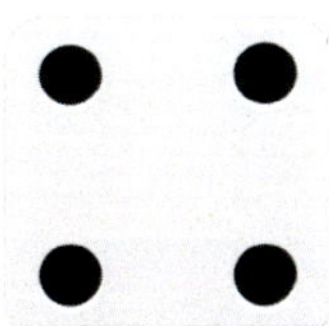 TOUCH YOUR TOES 10 TIMES

 DO 10 ARM CIRCLES

 DO 10 JUMPING JACKS

Reset Strategy 6: Music and Movement (Aleena, p. 34-35)

I Can Statement: *Like Aleena, I can practice music and movement as a reset strategy to help manage my emotions!*

Directions: Listen to different songs that make you feel good. Write down the name and artist of the songs you like best so you can come back to them again. You can also dance or just move to the songs while you are listening.

Music and Movement

My Playlist

Song Title	Artist

Reset Strategy 7: Visualization (Everly, p. 36-37)

I Can Statement: *Like Everly, I can practice* *__visualization__* *as a reset strategy to help manage my emotions!*

Directions: Read the prompt below and visualize your own story in your mind related to that prompt. Once you have visualized your story, use the boxes below to tell your story from start to finish.

Visualization

Tell Your Story

Imagine...
you are the first
person to discover
an island!

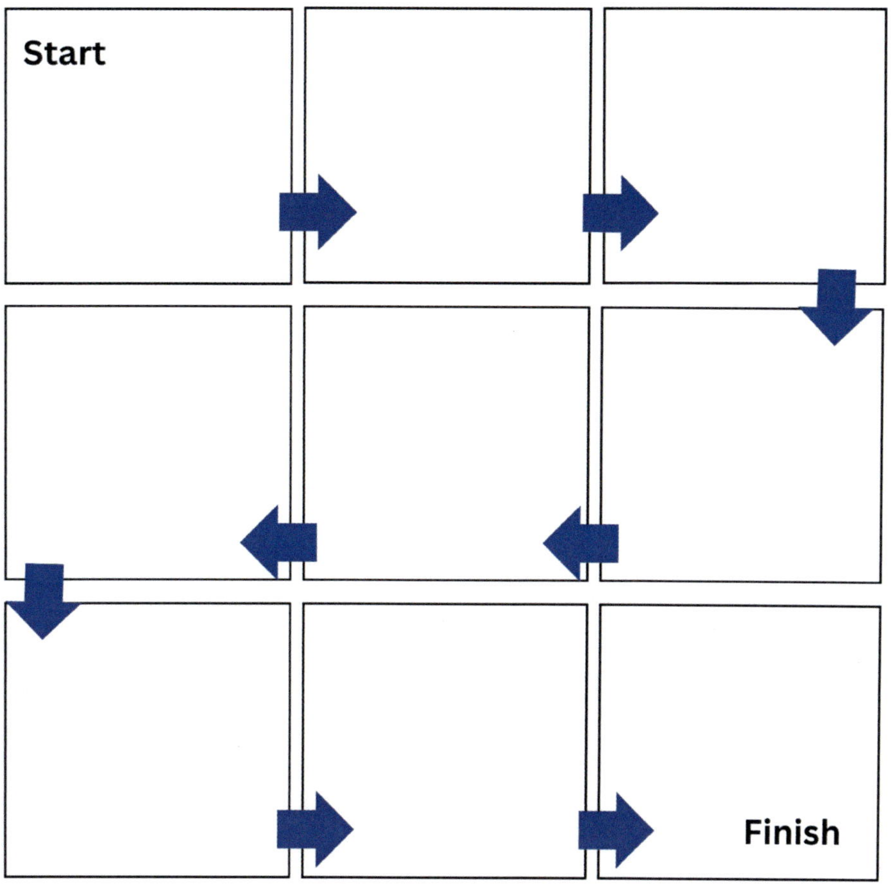

Reset Strategy 8: Guided Imagery (Mateo, p. 38-39)

I Can Statement: *Like Mateo, I can practice* *<u>guided imagery</u>* *as a reset strategy to help manage my emotions!*

Directions: Follow the directions below to imagine that you are a big and strong mountain. You can also think about your own story, like a favorite place you have been before or a favorite memory you have.

Guided Imagery

I am a Mountain

Step 1:
Close your eyes and picture the colors of a big, beautiful mountain. Pretend you are that mountain!

Step 2:
Stand up tall like your head is the tip of the mountain peak, reaching way up into the clouds.

Step 3:
Plant your feet firmly on the ground like they are the bottom of the mountain. Spread your toes out like rocks placed around the ground.

Step 4:
Imagine a river running through the mountain. Feel the nice, steady flow of water running over your feet.

Step 5:
Take a deep breath in like you are smelling the cool air. Now blow out like you are the wind around that mountain.

Step 6:
In your mind, picture as many details about this scene as you can. What else is there? What sounds do you hear? What else do you feel?

Reset Strategy 9: Talking to an Adult (Jordan, p. 40-41)

I Can Statement: *Like Jordan, I can practice <u>talking to an adult</u> as a reset strategy to help manage my emotions!*

Directions: Use the postcard below to write a note to an adult you trust, telling them how you are feeling right now and why you are feeling that way.

<u>Talking to an Adult</u>

<u>Greetings</u>

COLORING BOOK

Scan QR Code to Download the Coloring Book (P. 64-73)

Emily

Antonne

Jacob

Mika

Miya

Aleena

Everly

Mateo

Jordan

HERE'S TO HAPPY!

Made in the USA
Middletown, DE
18 November 2024

64685062R00046